IT IS GOING TO BE A GOOD YEAR

It Is Going To Be A Good Year
© 2016 Sasha Fletcher

Published by Big Lucks Books
Washington, DC
BigLucks.com

ISBN: 978-1-941985-04-5

Book design by Mark Cugini
Cover photograph by Sean Cain
Cover concept by JD Scott

Titles set in Young Serif
Text set in Crimson

First edition, March 2016

it is going to be a
good year

sasha fletcher

BIG LUCKS BOOKS 2016

dear margaret ross,

this book took 5 years,
but i've known you
for 15 so you win.

— ben

because of Skyler

"I want to tell you / how much I love you / but I'm drowning in the sea of love."

-Phil Phillips

it is going to be a good year

A breeze whistles through the trees
that used to be telephone poles.
My heart is a landslide
I say out loud and nine out of ten landslides agree.

world series or bust

Our town is near the pier and the pier
is near the sea and the sea
is a pack of wild dogs
just tearing across the horizon
and waiting to be put down
and tucked in for the night. Lately
we've been thinking about the word LONESOME
and twenty-one gun salutes
and how we want to see sacks of bones swinging
from trees and also we want a river
that'll run right through this town and drown us all
and then in the morning we want new bodies
and a diner and a parking lot and a drive-through cinema
and we want sunsets as far as the eye can see
and we want them now. Also
we want a sports team.
We want a championship sports team
and the World Series
and five hundred children and just yesterday
we were sitting at the table, eating dinner,
when you said Last night I saw this movie
where something wonderful happens,
where there's this beautiful woman staying up all night long
stitching birds to her boyfriend's back
and in the morning those birds they're gone so that night
they drive out to the parking lot on the edge of town

and turn on their headlights
and dance real slow while the radio sings
some sad songs of love and longing, and then they watch
as a lightning bolt tears the whole world apart,
and then their ghosts put on sheets and hold hands
on the boardwalk, terrifying the passersby until the end of time.
They loved each other very much,
and that was the end of the movie.
What else did you think would happen?

this is the year where astonishing things try to kill us

There are days I feel like waking up and discovering
I am pretty enough
to be strapped to the prow of a ship. You know?
Anyway if you've ever dreamed
of being pretty enough to be strapped to the prow of a ship
raise your hand. Otherwise proceed to the bank
where there will be men with bandanas for jaws
waiting to rob you blind and it is here, at this very bank,
with a gun in your face and your heart
attempting to escape out your mouth that you'll finally realize
that this is what love feels like, and, right now,
you are experiencing the single most important moment
in your entire life.

a love story

a love story

I walked right up to you and said Hello,
I am a bank robber and this is a robbery
so please give me all of the piles of money
in easy to carry bags. If you don't
I'll shoot you, and if you make a fuss
I'll shoot you in the face, and if you call the cops
then I'll shoot your whole entire body so full of bullets
that all of your blood will flee your body
like orphans fleeing from an orphanage
that's burning to the ground
and the orphans are screaming because they are on fire
and then they too burn to the ground
right there, in front of the TV cameras. If you'd like,
we could talk about our childhoods!,
we could go out for a cheeseburger
and pretend none of this ever happened,
and I could tell you a story
about a handsome man who meets a beautiful woman
at a bank. In her spare time
she falls deliriously in love with him
and they start a family together
and soon they have five hundred children
who all die in a flood. The handsome man
tells the beautiful woman
that everything will be OK. He tells her
that they loved their children very much

and that even though all of their children are now dead
that doesn't change their love. He tells her
she should really put all that money in some easy to carry bags
and then hand him those bags. Right now.
He says In two days you'll find me hiding in your bathroom
with a gun. He says I will tell you that your husband
is beginning to suspect something
and you will tell me that I am your husband
and immediately this will become true.

almost killed me

In the morning I was pinned to the ground by several birds.
You came into the kitchen and said Well this is a development.
The world was full of some kind of awful wonder
while outside a marching band struck up a parade
and then the refrigerator set itself on fire again
and after that things proceeded to get real interesting.

you are a beauty and i am alright

I told you to pretend that I was attractive
and it worked. You took my hand in yours
and we walked to the punch bowl
and punched someone in the mouth.
We went for the easy joke with pride
and we went for the door
with great purpose. After that
we started a life built on punch lines
in that I'll love you forever and then one day you'll die.
There's a radio in the corner
and it's playing static all night long
because that's the only station we like
and there are whole nights
where I could pull my limbs off
because I just love you so much
while upstairs the night sky is a stampede of horses
that are coming right for us
and then they do, trampling unto death absolutely everything
standing between us and certain doom,
and the whole world collapses around us
and we finally learn the meaning of love!
It was right there in front of us the whole time!
It was so obvious
that I'm not even going to talk about it.

when i go to bed i go to bed with the lights on

Every morning I look up at the moon and I think
You are a kiddie-pool and I will drown in you
and after that I think about field trips and cold cuts.
I think about dividends and other words
I don't understand. I make five hundred
lunches in advance. I want to be prepared.
I want new shoes. I want them to be waterproof
and unforgettable. I want the kind of resume
that takes home all the prizes plus a job offer
you wouldn't believe. I want to believe
that there are people in this world
whose lives are the size of houses. When I close my eyes
I can feel my heart. It's trembling.

In this movie I pull a raised platform strung up with lights
from out my mouth with zero difficulty
and then I stand on the stage and wait
while a crowd gathers and says What are you doing?
and I tell them that I am performing miracles. I start
by placing all their troubles in my mouth
until the world seems brighter
and this brightness is directly related
to the lights on my stage. I receive wild
and unheralded applause. At the edge of town
is a vast encroaching darkness.
Can you swallow that too they say
and I tell them I can swallow that too. Soon after
I retire. I build a house in the country
and read many books. Every day
I awake at dawn and take my coffee and bask
in my seclusion. There are tulips on the table
and I remain dissatisfied. Later that afternoon
I raise up an army of the dead and gather them in the woods.
We prepare to march on the town.
My army of the dead doesn't ask questions
and I like that about them.
We are getting excited. We are practicing our dance routines
and death. Pretty soon
it's a real horror show out here. My army of the dead
takes offense at the term "Horror Show"

but I don't tolerate insubordination
so I bury them in the ground. After that
I throw sheets over everything in the house.
I tell the gathering crowd that these are what we in the business call
"ghosts." They ask me what I plan on doing about these ghosts.
I tell them nothing.

date night

You called me up and asked me how things were going
and I told you that today I did something totally awesome
and entirely unfeasible and you said the sound of a pause
that was pregnant with all sorts of things
and so I said Hey I love you
and you said I love you too and then we both hung up.
When you came home you said How was the rest of your day?
and I told you that after we both hung up on our feelings
which remain hanging by their necks in the ether for all eternity
I went outside
where I felt like the sky was going to come crashing down
all over our heads,
laying waste to everything that ever happened,
but instead a light shone down upon me
in such ways as I'd never before seen.
You said Oh! You mean like a ghost?
and I said that the thing about ghosts
is that they are either people wearing bed sheets over their heads
and moaning all the time because they are too sad to live
or else they are just spooky as hell.
The ghosts behind us said We heard that
and we told them to shut it and stop being so sad
and that is exactly what they did
and everyone in the whole world suddenly felt better.
Over night I made a whole entire fortune via bank robbery
or at least enough for us to go out and have a nice dinner

and drink buckets of margaritas.
This is really something wonderful you said
and I agreed. I told you
that I loved you very much
and everyone at the restaurant agreed and after that
we went home and got into bed
and talked about the future
in that I said In the future after the world ends
we'll all be ghosts
and the ghosts in the living room said Like us?
And I said Shut up ghosts I'm telling a story
and they did. I said We'll be ghosts
with sheets for faces and BOOs for lungs
and we'll walk around the beach
while up in the sky pink thunderclouds
start screaming their heads off. I'm not saying
this is a masterpiece. But I'm not saying it isn't.
Across the boardwalk
is a band with some serious backing vocals
and we're swaying there in the breeze
and the crowds are parting around us,
and the thunderclouds keep screaming
and screaming, and the whole sky starts clapping
and weeping at our love, which is a beacon, and a lighthouse,
and something that has some serious plans for the future
as we make our way to the moon, surveying all below us

as they throw flowers at our feet, and beg us to take a bow
but we don't, because we're too busy making out
which is a thing ghosts do
instead of bursting into a million pieces
and dispersing whatever is left of themselves
throughout all of humanity while the world explodes
because love is beautiful
and not at all an impossibility
and if this doesn't move you then that's just too fucking bad.

loud mouth

I am going to take you to the notary
and get you notarized. I plan to appear before you
as death itself
all dressed up like a skeleton
and riding into town on a skeleton horse
or some other form of dirt bike
and then I am going to sing to you. I am going to sing to you
about how I have never loved a soul before like I love you now
and other sweet nothings
is an album I am thinking of recording.
Its cover is going to be a picture of you
completely naked
and dressed up like a ghost.
This evening you stand before me like a vision of the days
when our hopes and dreams just tear themselves apart.
I mean picture this: The sun is rising up in the sky
and setting flame to the procession,
that one, right there,
and we are standing hand in hand
and promising each other things that will never be repeated
and I have put five hundred children in your belly
and you are getting prettier by the minute
and we are in a speedboat sailing the asphalt seas of parking lots
with our five hundred children
each one of them somehow causing us to love
every one of them even more until our hearts

have grown other hearts to handle the load
and what more can we say here
except that the boat crashed and the children
were swallowed up by the parking lots
and they all died and we never saw them ever again
and that's the best way I can think
to describe how I feel when I look at you.

progress report

I have not memorized the books of the Bible
and I've never performed a miracle
and I couldn't spell Monongahela
without looking it up in a book
and I DON'T EVEN KNOW
should be the title of the book
that I'm thinking of writing about myself.
I'm thinking of writing a book about myself.
I just want to be clear here.

we, the people

We are a slow moving cold front. We are shipwrecks
with legs and we go to sleep
at reasonable hours. At dusk we walk through the streets.
We look at the houses we've built of our lives.
We string up lights between them.
Our eyes have seen the glory
and this is it.

abide with me

Last night I swear I saw a coffin sailing down the asphalt
like that movie where this guy drags a coffin around
for someone to die in. I have to say
it moved me. If you were to ask
if there was another way to say this
then you would be wrong. Out here there are ghosts
everywhere if you know how to look. These days
I want to tell you how much I love you
and find it to be absolutely impossible. These days
I keep my feelings in my pockets with my liquor and insecurities.
I keep my finger on the chicken
because I'm always getting hungry
for chicken, or a good job, or your unending affection. These days
I'm working on this speech. It goes: The asphalt
is a sea and I will part it. Furthermore:
This is the kind of parking lot
a man could drown in, so come on in boys, the water is fine.
And then they do.
There's a crowd now. They've entered the scene
and it's a damned shame you only just noticed them.
They're up to their necks in it,
and singing, soft and low, like a hymn. These days
there are armed revolts in our hearts every day of the week.
Don't talk to me about anything other than love.
Please.

the state of the union

The president came on the radio and told us
that life was, at times, a very difficult and painful event
that will basically always end in death. The president said,
however,
that we are all winners if we try hard enough
and it is difficult, he knows!, to choose kindness, but who says
that kindness is not, in this day and age, a radical act? Life
said the president Is a form of revolt if you do it right
and that was the end of the president's announcement. After that
everyone got health insurance and after that
everyone died, because woe is me, as casually as possible.

my heart is an ice floe and it will wreck you

We were sitting in the kitchen making dinner
when the radio started telling us all about how polar bears
were slowly moving across the arctic circle, headed
inevitably towards warmer climates
and our still-beating hearts, which call out to them
like an all-night buffet. I told you
No polar bear is going to eat the still-beating heart
of the woman I love as long as I live
and you said that that was really sweet
so I dove into the sea. Eventually
I found myself in the Arctic. It was cold
so I put on a sweater. I lay down on the ground
with my mouth open and I waited. When a polar bear came by
I closed my mouth down around its leg
and I said Now you are trapped
and the polar bear bled all over my face and died!
I built a home in the polar bear's stomach
and I built a fire in my home in the polar bear's stomach
and walked on out of that home with a year's supply of dinner.
That night I was surrounded
by a pack of polar bears seeking vengeance.
A pack of polar bears is actually called an aurora
but there's nothing menacing about an aurora,
so I fled across the ice and commandeered an iceberg
with which I set sail for your smiling face
until I shipwrecked some sailors. There I was!,

adrift in the Arctic, surrounded
by the broken bodies of shipwrecked sailors,
every one of them weeping and bleeding and begging to die,
so I built a ship from their bones and off I went
into the sunset with the wind at my back
while that ship just cried and cried and cried.
I asked the ship to stop that.
I said Stop that. Nobody cares about your sadness
I sang to that ship and it cried and it cried and it cried
and a children's choir five hundred strong joined in
and we all sang out Nobody cares about your sadness
and we all kept singing and singing and singing
until the sky broke open and the curtain dropped
and the broken hearted wives of the shipwrecked sailors
drowned us in applause.

i am afraid at times of the stories i tell

In my free time I build altars. Recently I built you one
inside my locker. It consists of you
inside my locker. I have arranged around it some candles
and a bag of takeout. It would mean a lot to me
if you'd make a face like a burning building.
If you'd like to get a drink, circle yes.
If you heard that I am blessed with a gentle disposition
on certain days then you heard right. You should know
that my favorite activity is when I take my troubles
and I bury them in your mouth. I call this making out
and we can do it all night. You tell me
you've heard all this before
and then you walk on out my locker and you go to work.
You call me up. I tell you I love you. You tell me
Across the street a bird is dragging the carcass of a deer
across the road. Five hundred children sit in stadium seating
and watch wearing sheets with the eyes cut out like ghosts,
and then the wind blows like a sharp intake of breath, revealing
that beneath their sheets are five hundred piles of bones
saying BOO over and over again, first softly
and then louder, and then louder, and then louder
and louder and louder and louder and louder
and louder, until it is the only sound in the entire world.

torch song

I had been shoveling snow into the sea
because I was worried. I was weeping.
I was standing on the pier and I was waiting
for something wonderful to happen
but I got tired of waiting
so I left. I was walking through the grocery store
as it was trying to close. I felt like the cashier
was staring right at me.
I felt like a shoplifter. I felt like a bandit.
I felt like I was holding a loaded gun or a gallon
of milk. We were in Mexico and I was a loaded gun
and the way you wrapped your hands around me
made me tremble and shake. There were fireworks
everywhere I could see. On the radio
a song was playing. I saw the city
all decked out in lights
from the inside of a fort. I was in a fort
and I was holding things down.
I was in a bank. I was telling everyone
I had only the best of intentions. I cannot say
if this was true. I was riding a horse
into the sunset. I told it not to ruin the moment.
I was standing in front of a lawn
warding off loneliness
like a real pro. I was moving

like a shipwreck. I went out to the beach
and sat down in a chair and the tide
swallowed me whole. I was standing on the pier.
I was just standing there. In the distance was a marching band.
It was stirring and alive and then it stopped.

i love you

I am going to take your hand in mine and just hold it there
and you are going to have to deal with that.
I am going to buy you a plant
because I want to brighten your day and also
because it is going to try to kill you
and you are going to have to deal with that
and if that doesn't work we can just set ourselves on fire
and wake up on a desert island where the moon hangs real low
and the sea is as vast and endless a harbinger of certain doom
as our love, which is the kind of thing you could drown in.
I want to tell you something real important.
I swear to god.

act nice and gentle

I am not a fancy man it is true but that does not mean
that I do not own a suit or understand how to open doors
or prevent ladies from stepping in puddles. The best way
to prevent ladies from stepping in puddles
is to drown the puddle and bury it in a shallow grave
over by the orphanage. The best way to cheer up an orphan
is to take the orphan out for a cheeseburger
and point out that there is no such thing as "parents."
Often after improving the lives of ladies and orphans
I like to go out into the woods and take out my wallet
and see if I can make rent this month
and it is indeed the best of games!
I would like to take the time here to remind you
that I have got a tenderness in me that cannot be contained
and also there is not a moment that goes by
wherein I do not imagine that you are right here,
nestling against my neck, and the sun is setting
and the trees are swaying in a comfortable breeze
and we can have a good time, we could get margaritas,
we could have a mutual suicide pact
that involved massive explosions
and guns mounted on the ceiling that fire when we sigh,
severing cords tied to bowling balls that will crush our heads
and yes I have been feeling sorry for myself
and when you get off work tonight
I would like you to sit here with me, on the couch,

while the freeway tells us a real good joke
and we all laugh together like the good old days,
because darlin I am nothing
if not a living reminder of the good old days
which we have drowned and buried
out by the orphanage, where hope lives in secret,
burrowing itself inside you so deep
that you almost forget it's there.

bedtime stories

Once upon a time there was a guy with a real great haircut
and one day he was elected President of the Unites States
and then promptly lost his oldest son, his wife,
his Vice President, the rest of his children,
his nomination for re-election
and his lunch money and after that he buried himself
inside a bottle of gin while vultures
fed on the remains of everything he ever lost,
as was the custom of the time
is the sort of bedtime story about America I'd want to tell you
and the five hundred children you'll never let me give you
and when I tell you this
I'll be smiling, because your life is a shining example
of all the things I have never done, and if I could
I would replace everyone's face with yours so that every day
my heart would just break wide open and burst into flames
and I would, in that moment,
be completely surrounded by your love
right before my head explodes in a miraculous tribute
to this great nation, and we wake up in the morning
and do it all over again, but different, and better,
with a car crash, a shipwreck, a close encounter
with certain doom, several semi-successful bank robberies,
and a truly spectacular excuse for a dinner party,
with the sort of twist ending that just sends you staggering out,
cold and wild, into that dark night

just waiting for destiny
to manifest itself all over your broken, anxious face.

i have often thought of you as a sort of mountaintop or peak

I know that you have got a switchblade for a heart but listen
that's just fine with me because I don't even have a heart
so there is no basis for comparison in this situation.

crybaby

The world famous motel singers have got something to tell me
at least that's what they keep insisting
with their sequined tops swaying in the breeze while here I am
sitting in the driver's seat
eating up some takeout
and wishing you were here with me
parked in front of this Ferris wheel
that is functionally on fire. Nostalgia gets the better of me
and I regret that. You appear as if out of nowhere
or the trunk. The motel singers come on the radio
to a thunderous applause that would shake a baby unto death
and you immediately arm a dozen nuclear missiles
and tell me that they can only be disarmed by genuine remorse,
which is a concept I have always had some trouble with
and o!, how I have missed the way
you carve your name on my face when you kiss me
right on my loud mouth!, but so anyway
I shoot the missiles down using my feelings or a handgun
and you ask me what that was all about. I tell you
that I am just waiting for something wonderful to happen.
You ask me what exactly I mean by that,
launching a volley of birds
who pin me to the ground and I tell you
that I don't know what "something wonderful" means,
but I'm pretty sure it sounds magnificent,
like that time we dressed up as bandits

and walked into the bank and took everyone's money
and made every single person there fall in love with us
and then we shot them full of holes and folded
what remained into airplanes
and mailed them straight to heaven
and then we moved into an empty apartment and went to sleep
happy. That night while I slept
you stitched trees to my back and sold me
to the city as a small forest or park
and then, after the check cleared,
that small forest or park burned to the ground
under "mysterious circumstances," and after that
I woke up. I went to the hospital
where I received a brand new back
that was fireproofed, and gleaming.
The kind and gentle nurses
told me to maybe start thinking
about possibly even taking it easy
and I smiled at them as long as I could
because I am not impolite
and then I got into a car and I drove out to our apartment,
and you walked out the door
and told me you'd missed me
and shot my leg in the leg. I grew a new one
using my feelings and it,
like my feelings,

has got your name carved on its face
because that's how we talk about making out.
You asked me if I remembered the time you buried me alive
and told everyone that I was what killed the dinosaurs.
I told you about this movie I'd seen,
the one where something wonderful happens.
You said that you had never seen anything like that
and I said I'd take you to see it
and then I stuffed you in the trunk
while the radio sang a song just for you
with pedal steel guitars and weeping women
and the world's smallest violin. All I ever wanted
was for us to find some common ground and build a life upon it.
You tell me you know just what I mean. Meanwhile
I am begging you,
and the motel singers are begging you,
and the polar bears are begging you,
and the sea of love is begging you,
and my unappeasable sadness is begging you,
and god is begging you, and the ghosts are begging you,
and the president!,
the president is begging you,
and our five hundred children are begging you,
and we are, at this very moment, cueing up the strings
and the whole world is holding its breath.

real love

When you came home I was in the kitchen doing the dishes
like a champion. When you came home you said
You look nice tonight
and I said Thanks, because I was, essentially,
everything anyone could ever want. I kissed you
right on your mouth which was on your face
in the front of your head. The ghosts out the window
were arrayed like a studio audience
but their reactions remained difficult to understand. Apparently
they were delivering unto us a vast and thunderous applause
and the skies were parting to bathe us in such heavenly light
indicating that the end was coming over and over again and I said
Would you like to hear a good joke?,
and you said Yes, and then the sky fell down,
and, because every story needs an ending, this one ends
with massive explosions that shake the very fabric of our being,
during a terrible car crash, at sea, while ghosts
are carted on up to heaven by presidential decree,
and we hold hands like the only people who ever knew love,
and are survived by our five hundred children
who have, of their own accord, left directions
for our tombstone to read SAVIORS OF ALL MANKIND.

these are the days of glory

You and me get in a real championship of a prizefight
which is a term we made up for when the whole world drowns
and the World Series gets won and lost and our lives
take on the size of the sort of houses we can afford on this budget
and then, late at night, we take off our skin
and we dance as the good lord intended
for these, right here, are the days of glory.
I want you to sit here, and let me tell you all about how I love you.
I want to tell you something wonderful. I want to tell you
about how, with you by my side, how could I fail?,
except spectacularly, in the grand tradition
of our five hundred children,
and our five hundred children's children,
in such a way that failure itself ceases to exist
and all that's left is the sampler on the wall
that says PLEASE COME AGAIN SOON?

the night is long and difficult

At my door there was a knock and I opened it
and in front of me was a policeman.
He said Hello. He said It is real cold out
and I'm pretty sure he was totally telling the truth
because there was a foot of snow standing on top of him
due to a sudden snowstorm
that really took us all by surprise. I invited him in
and he told me that he was investigating ghosts.
There had been he said Reports of ghosts in the area,
And the populace he told me
Was awful delicate, and frequently driven
towards outlandish and melodramatic demonstrations
of violence dressed up as love. He said I often worry
about what it feels like to be shot in the face.
He asked if I'd seen any ghosts
and I said What and then Yes and he said Where
so I said Out the window, frequently moaning or singing,
bearing witness to the world like a studio audience
or a bunch of ghosts.
He told me that that sounded like ghosts alright.
He told me that earlier today he was in the bathroom
of a bank, having investigated a robbery,
as there have been a real rash of them of late,
and as he came out of the stall he was surrounded
on all sides
by what appeared to be ghosts

and so he called out Disperse ghosts!
This bathroom is no place for you!
and so I asked him what happened next
and He said What do you think?
so I told him that the thing about ghosts
is that they are either people wearing bed sheets over their heads
and moaning all the time because they are too sad to live
or else they are some sort of supernatural mystery
impossible to explain away with science
or the powers of observation
or an enormous handgun. The world is full of things
that we can never fully prepare for.
Life is a mystery he said to me
And everyone dies alone. Then he walked himself out the door
and down the street. He goes home to his wife
and looks at her
like he hasn't seen her in years.
(Meanwhile all of the lights in the whole world
turn off and we're all of us bathed in darkness
and it's great.) Their whole lives become wrapped
in a gigantic bed sheet of longing,
and their mouths press together
doing something more than kissing
and some weird kind of light emerges from inside them,
and it grows brighter and brighter and brighter and brighter
and brighter

until there's nothing left between them anymore.
Nothing but light. Out the window are the ghosts.
In the sky is the moon. I'm at home, with the lights off,
watching a movie
where a man meets a beautiful woman, and they fall in love,
and it doesn't work out, and then there's a murder mystery,
but in the end almost nobody dies, justice is served,
and love, though sometimes fleeting,
is something to be real grateful for
even when it makes you want to shoot yourself in the face.

my eyes have seen the dawning

When I woke up I didn't have a beard
so I made one out of paper
and I held it to my face. Look at my beard!
I said but you were eating oatmeal
and seemed unimpressed
so I cracked my mouth wide open and from it
came a vast and encroaching darkness
and in a moment it was night.

local news

The newspapers say I have got a real loud mouth,
and it's true!, but the newspapers have got nothing to say
about the fact that outside there are ghosts
being drawn in the air by lost children shouting BOO
and hoping for something wonderful to happen,
although I got five dollars that says they've got no idea
what that even means. Meanwhile
I'm out here piling up my regrets near the door
and waiting for the mailman to put them in his pocket
and leave me something wonderful. In the refrigerator
is a bunch of heartache. Today at the door
there was milk and tomorrow there'll be a thunderstorm
during which clouds will descend upon this house
and they'll yell real loud
and someone'll do something real drastic
and that someone will be me.

In this movie I am a whole entire gang of horse thieves
out stealing horses
(because we already robbed all the banks so there's no more banks)
who gets stopped by a man on horseback
who proceeded to try to tell me a thing or two about horse thievery
as though I didn't know a thing or two about horse thievery
so I took the man by his leg
and I beat him ten times against the ground
because I am a reasonable man
is the kind of joke we could tell
if we were the kind of people who liked jokes
and then his horse and I
we went all the way to Toledo
if that is even a real place
and that is where we met you, for the first time
at dawn. You said Are you a whole entire gang of horse thieves
and I said Obviously and then we got married
because I was exactly what you were looking for. In the morning
we had enough sex to make five hundred thousand children
and then we stole all of the horses
literally all of the fucking horses
and escaped entirely unnoticed
and then we got the fuck out of Toledo
for what we considered to be pretty obvious reasons
and we kept riding until we got to a place
where towns don't even have names,

and upon our arrival discovered
that there was not a single horse
as far as the eye could see.
We're talking about a real seller's market
such that we immediately became people of wealth and value
and our clothes were knit from the bones
of tired miners and when they wrote the Bible
do you think they could have imagined this
out here where the sun gets buried by the townsfolk each night
and everyone sits on the bench facing east
waiting to see what happens next?,
when, suddenly, a title card drops down from the heavens, proclaiming
WHAT HAPPENS NEXT: what happens next is
after we unload the horses
and receive our various compensations and fineries
we build a house out where the sun hides its face.
After that we have dinner.
For dinner we are having everything
and we are having it in bed. Our bed
is made out of gold and miracles
and something totally wonderful
which may or may not be the hair of many virgins.
We hear rumblings, but we pay them no mind.
What happens next is the townsfolk rise up
and smother our dreams
which is a word we just invented

to describe our feelings
which are vast
and choke this very land
with their brilliance and magnitude.

are you kidding me

Today my resume feels alive with purpose.
What does that mean exactly? I couldn't say.
If I were to think about it my head would explode,
and then you would have to deal with that.
It's just something I've come to believe,
like how some days the sun rises in the east and on others
we continue our never-ending plea for some great event
which we will recognize as occurring once the strings kick in
and the narrator warmly and wisely intones
It was then that they fully understood their purpose in life,
retired to the country, and lived happily ever after
but friends, until then, let's burn everything to ground
and keep it that way
until all that we can see is dead and gone
and we are finally alone with our feelings
which we are absolutely terrified of.

this is why we can't have nice things

I am going to build you an island and you are going to love it.
I am going to carve your face into a mountain
and then I am going to buy you a present. It is going to be a cat
and you are going to love it
or it'll die and that'll be all your fault and you'll feel terrible
and feeling terrible is real inconvenient
because when you feel terrible the bandits come
and they live in your closet and at night while you sleep
they shoot off your face and they set your children on fire
and they peel the skin from everything you ever loved
and they nail it to your door in the shape of your sadness.

a vast and shining piece of beauty

There are whole days I want to leap into traffic
because that's how I get in the mood for love.
According to the radio
my favorite disguise is when I change my mind.
At the grocery store dinner was on sale
so I bought some and I really hope they work out.
At night the sky gets dark
but you already knew that.

feel good event of the summer

The president decreed that we the people
should try not to feel terrible so that bandits
do not come and cut off our faces to wear as masks
while they kidnap our children and raise them as their own.
The president said Our children are a national treasure.
He said Our children are the gilded icebergs of our hearts.
He said Who wants fireworks? And we all said I DO.

in the mood for love

Everyone finally had a good year, briefly, and without incident.
I dressed up as the sky because the sky is a lake
and it will swallow you, because obviously, because these days
the sea of love is just another movie theater
showing stories about how we're the greatest thing ever,
and now here we are!, with our blood on fire!, and drowning!,
in the sea of love!,
which is how we talk about making out
because I look so good in this suit.

the sea of love

The moon continued to sit in the sky like a fucking liar.
Our fingers itched for triggers
we would never know. Tears
flowed down our faces
just like the policeman said they would. The snow fell
like an apology. An apology
is the worst way to say I love you
out here in the sea of love, which we are drowning in,
and it is just plain terrible! When lo! The waters part!,
revealing every mistake we ever made
dressed up as a thundering thunder cloud all in black,
and the size of a minivan, and made of lightning and also death,
and headed straight for us, and calling our names,
which are you, and me. And it's not that I'm not sorry.
It's just that I want to love you
like a pile of bones.

i'm sorry

You said Listen I'm not saying that you're wrong but I am saying
that in the morning when you wake you'll find yourself
completely alone and unable to love anything at all
because you would just hate that,
and I told you that that sounded right,
and you told me
that that was how the world sounded when I talked to you
But don't make a big deal out of it you said.
You said Or I mean, make a big deal out of it,
see the kind of trouble it gets you,
you said What it gets you is it gets you burnt at the stake,
you said When we talk about witchcraft
you should know that it's not what you think.
You said I'm not saying your life is a hangable offense
but I'm not not saying it either, is the punch line here,
and then you kissed me, right on the mouth.
You said Baby I didn't mean it. You said Baby
I love you. You said When I look at you
I just want to swaddle you in blankets
and feed you whiskey from a bottle
and pretend you are a cupcake
and swallow you whole. You said But baby
that doesn't mean you're not going to die here.
You said Dear ghosts out the window you said
Right? You said Back me up here.
You said Please. And the ghosts out the window got this look

like Really? Are you really going to bring up sudden
and inevitable death to a fright of ghosts?
Because listen, there are stories we could tell you
if you had any idea how to begin to listen to a story
that does not directly concern you, and these stories
would unfold before your hearts like a major motion picture
taking home all of the awards while you crumble to your knees
in the manner of a fine character actor
who is, in fact, no longer acting. Once upon a time said the ghosts
There was a dimly lit highway
in the dead of night, and the highway got real lonely,
and never did anything about it
because what kind of person ever really bothers to fight for love?
THE END goes the big sign dropped in front of us
and proclaiming THE END
as the house lights go up and the strings play us out
but the ghosts kept going because the thing about ghosts
is that they are impervious to context clues,
because the world is an ever-shifting collection
of facts and fictions and right now
this very instant snow is falling in every direction
and it has turned the river into an ice rink
which a pile of children are skating upon
because everything, and we mean *everything*,
is a hangable offense if you do it right
is one way of looking at this world.

Our life is not a movie and you are a dead man is another,
and either way here is a pretty good joke:
So one ghost turns to the other and says
Listen I know that we're just ghosts
of the memory of a feeling someone once had
but I know deep down that I can't think of a single thing
I'd rather do than float around
and be a spooky pile of wonder with you
for forever
and I know that some days you feel the same way
and on others your heart is promised to a former president
living with all the other former presidents forever and ever
under the White House in a house made entirely of diamonds
and muttering spells spelled out in blood in his off hours,
and I know that eventually
the two of you will go on to live a full and wonderful life
where you're mostly completely happy,
and on two separate occasions
you'll think of me, fondly,
as a knife made entirely of sadness just misses your throat
because lord knows! But that's it. That's the end.

In this movie I'm in the grocery store
whose radio is beyond our control
and I'm dressed up like a real employee-of-the-month situation
who has got some things to tell you about
like how the other day someone came in acting like a bandit
and so that is exactly how I looked at him
and the gallon of milk clutched in his fist.
I'd like to tell you about the sale on milk
in that tomorrow all unsold milk will be taken out back and shot.
I'd like to tell you about the soup. How the soup tastes
is vulnerable. These days the days grow longer
and the nights die off. Out in our parking lot
are the mothers both unwed and wed.
They are waiting there in tribute to the memory
of their last important battle cry, which is as follows:
IT DOES NOT MATTER HOW MANY TIMES
YOU TELL US WE ARE AMAZING
BECAUSE WE KNOW IT IN OUR HEARTS
BUT THAT DOES NOT MEAN WE DO NOT APPRECIATE IT.
SO SAYETH THE BATTLE AXE they say,
lifting their battle axes from out their skirts
dividing up the light of the grocery store amongst themselves
and placing it next to their hearts, for in their hearts
it is always the World Series, and death is on the line,
and in a situation like that we are all in need
of a well-lit place to die in.

while you were out

I am writing this note to tell you
that our five hundred children have been stolen by bandits
from right under our noses. We assumed
that a safe deposit box was a good place to keep them
but I guess we were wrong. I have alerted the police
and they are doing what they can. Dear bandits
when you stole our children did you realize
you have to feed them three times a day?
Do you have any idea what sort of budget that will require?
Dear bandits you should be aware that our five hundred children
are full of book learning and a quiet desperation
that will terrify your insides right out of your body
and there you'll be!, on the floor!,
with your insides terrified right out of your body
and wishing with all your life that you had any idea
how to love anything at all. But wait! There's more!
Everything will go silent. The ghosts will come calling.
They'll say terrible things about you. They'll tell you
you were the worst men who ever lived.
They'll pack your terrified insides
into fireworks that, when lit, amount to absolutely nothing at all.
What? Did you think you'd die
in the kind of way they'd write poems about?

let me tell you about my day

Today you got up and went to work after leaving our bed
and our bedroom and our apartment, in that order,
going out into the wide world,
collecting all of the awards and being compensated
in money and also the furs of your enemies
whose jawbones I have removed, and am currently wearing
as a symbol of my office. Today
I took off my skin and let my bones
take the air. Today I attempted two minor miracles
and although they were unsuccessful,
they remained remarkable. Today
I want to tell you how these days it is getting harder
and harder to tell you just how much I love you.
I want to tell you some other things, too. I mean
I think about things other than love
is a really good joke I could tell the ghosts out the window.
What do you do these days?
ask the ghosts at the window. I tell them
I am keeping a clean house. What are you doing now?
they ask. I tell them
I AM INCREASING MY CAPACITY FOR LOVE
in letters ten feet high, and on fire. And as soon as I do,
everything falls away.
I mean every single thing I could see just fell away
and all that was left was the window
and the ghosts behind it
and then we all fell to the ground.

i seem to be doing alright

Last night we went to a dinner party. Most of the guests
hadn't seen each other in a while
and were taking turns remembering
why they hadn't kept in touch
and everyone was awkwardly talking about unemployment
or their last bad decision
like these five hundred children
who were holding the hands of their parents and looking up
as though this moment was going to change their lives forever!,
when suddenly the sky went completely dark
and we were surrounded, on all sides, by trees.
Where did all these trees come from
is what everyone was asking, but we had no answers.
Then the trees broke everyone's limbs
and we were lying there all broken and bleeding
and the skulls of our five hundred children
were gaping up at us in piles on the floor.
Then the president came and he put a stop to things
with his two big hands and his full, bright heart
and we said Wow thank you that was a miracle
and he said Don't mention it
and we never did. The next day the weather began to change
and this change in the weather was voted
as being real inconvenient
but apparently voting doesn't do anything
because the weather continued to suck,
and so then when the river froze over

we went out and had a picnic on it
while a movie was projected onto the ever-falling snow
and, for a moment, it seemed like there were angels
coming down to greet us and I couldn't stop smiling,
but then the movie stopped and you were gone,
and it was just me and the picnic blanket,
and the picnic blanket was stuck to the frozen river,
and then I was completely alone. In my head
you'd realized that it made more sense
to maybe just finally have had enough
but honestly probably during the movie
you were abducted by those malicious and bloodthirsty trees
from that truly spectacular excuse for a dinner party
and they snapped your limbs off every night forever
and whenever I thought about any of this it just tore me to pieces.
A breeze whistled through the trees
and that just tore me to pieces. So there I was,
on the floor of our apartment, torn to pieces
and completely alone. On the radio someone sang a song
and I did not care for that song at all
and then the president interrupted the song
which was a totally great move on the president's part
and the president then apologized for the weather
and for the loneliness that had descended upon this great nation
like a wet wool blanket,
completely isolating us from anyone and anything

we had ever loved. The president told us
that soon blood would fall from the sky
and the trees would eat our houses whole
and we'd all flee to the mountains and pray
for a sudden and painless death,
but death would not come, and we'd live like that,
forever. I had mixed feelings
regarding the president's announcement
so I pulled myself together and got up off the floor.
I walked out the back door
of our third floor walk-up and went out to the yard
where I found a pig and I shot it in the head and I chopped it up
into pork chops, which I fried on the stove,
and they were absolutely delicious. The sun,
which had not been seen since that spectacular excuse
for a dinner party earlier,
was reflected off of my face in ways
that were truly staggering.
Several bits of me gleamed. The weather patterns
maintained a holding position, you remained
out of pocket, the world continued to spin,
gradually exhausting itself and all of its resources,
and our apartment was full of balloons
that said, loudly, WELCOME HOME I MISSED YOU.
They are here still, waiting for you to pop them.
In the meantime

I have my pork chops and I have my loneliness
and I see no reason these will not last me through the winter
which promises to be cold, and unending!

new year's eve

I don't know if you've noticed
but things have gotten a little oppressive over here!
The sadness! It is everywhere and we are choking on it!
We are on our knees! It is very dramatic!
I have some things to say about the above situation,
and they are as follows: We're over it. We are, in fact,
at this very moment, contemplating a serious change,
something new and wonderful
that will fill our hearts with not just satisfaction, but purpose,
the kind of purpose shaped like a minivan
and composed entirely of certain doom and headed
right for us. And so what! Who cares! Dear everybody
Please be quiet. The movie is starting, right now,
and it's starring the handsome couple! They are on a date!
They are on a date and eating dinner
when the restaurant suddenly catches on fire and the firemen
are nowhere to be found and a lightning bolt tears the night sky
right in half, and both halves collapse to the ground,
and just like that it's over, and it's winter,
and it's poignant, and the snow is falling, and that's us!, the snow,
falling, at night, that's all we have to do here
is fall. Soon there are piles of snow like hip high mountains
and the sky is this deep purple and the moon
is huge, I mean it's enormous,
I mean it could just swallow us whole.

if i was trying to break your heart i'd have already done it

After a while I disappear into the narrative
or the woods. Eventually
our five hundred children repair to a clearing
in the center of the aforementioned woods.
They turn on their TV's and try not to stare at the moon
which is looming, ominously, in the corner,
making it very clear that it is coming for us all,
altering the tides and also the minds of the populace,
as the air fills up with ghosts,
like the kind of movie you just can't wait to see.

This is the movie where something wonderful happens.
In this movie we rent a cabin and spend whole days together
and our ribs shatter because our hearts have grown so large
and it's a real blood bath in that we're taking a bath
in all this blood, and it's real romantic. Then there's a lake
and the lake is a real blood bath
in that whatever is in there was slaughtered to death.
I'm just kidding! It's all this blood from our hearts.
In this movie I finally tell you how much I love you.
I say it with a three-car pile up.
I say it with a fireplace and a 401K. I say it
as indirectly as possible. Then the angels come.

and then we come back for an encore

love is real

We are standing on the pier trying to watch the sunset
but it's not there. Instead there are ships
wrecking themselves all over the place. We applaud
wildly. They come up for a bow. All around us
are candles. It is incredibly romantic. We are no longer afraid
of death or money. We want to watch the sunset now
but the sky does not oblige us. We want to watch the sunset
we say out loud. All we want is the sunset
the sunset the sunset the sunset the sunset
the sunset the sunset the sunset the sunset
the sunset the sunset the sunset the sunset
the sunset the sunset the sunset the sunset
the sunset the sunset the sunset the sunset
the sunset the sunset the sunset the sunset
the sunset the sunset the sunset the sunset
the sunset the sunset the sunset the sunset
the sunset

and the curtain drops to wild and unheralded applause

and that's it. that's the end.

Acknowledgments

Versions of these poems have appeared in *Big Lucks, Black Warrior Review, Bodega, Boston Review, Dark Sky Magazine, Day One, Death Hums, Glitter Mob, Poor Claudia, Crush, Powder Keg, Prelude, Red Lightbulbs, Sink Review, Sixth Finch,* and *Swarm.*

Thanks to Kirkwood Adams, Eric Amling, Skyler Balbus, Josh Bell, Melissa Broder, Jay Deshpande, Annie DeWitt, Tim Donnelly, Nalini and Josh Edwin, Ben Fama, Emily Kendal Frey, Amelia Gray, Catherine Lacey, Hilary Leichter, Monica McClure, Ben Mirov, Rebecca Novack, and Liz Clark Wessel for their friendship, support, and feedback. "something wonderful" is for Rebecca. Special bonus thanks to Kirkwood Adams and Josh Bell for the extra incessant last minute feedback. Endless thanks to Mark Cugini, my brother Nate, and my parents Les and Lucy, for their unending belief, love, support, and enthusiasm.